Faith,
HOMOSEXUALITY

A Report by the Evangelical Alliance's Commission
on Unity and Truth among Evangelicals (ACUTE)

Faith, Hope &
HOMOSEXUALITY

Copyright © 1998 Evangelical Alliance
Whitefield House, 186 Kennington Park Road, London SE11 4BT
Printed by Halcyon Print and Design

This edition printed in 1998 by Acute

04 03 02 01 00 99 98   7 6 5 4 3 2 1

Acute is an imprint of Paternoster Publishing,
P.O. Box 300, Carlisle, Cumbria, CA3 0QS, U.K.
http:www.paternoster-publishing.com

British Library Cataloguing in Publication Data
A catalogue record for this book is available from the British Library.
ISBN 0-9532992-0-1

Cover Design by Mainstream, Lancaster
Typeset by WestKey Ltd, Falmouth, Cornwall
Printed in Great Britain by Mackays of Chatham PLC, Kent

Contents

About ACUTE

ACUTE is the Evangelical Alliance's Commission on Unity and Truth among Evangelicals. It exists to work for consensus on theological and other issues which test evangelical unity, and seeks on behalf of evangelicals to provide a coordinated theological response to matters of wider public debate.

As well as Evangelical Alliance members, ACUTE's Steering Group includes representatives of the British Evangelical Council and the Evangelical Movement of Wales.

For more information about ACUTE write to: Rev Dr David Hilborn, Coordinator, ACUTE, Evangelical Alliance, Whitefield House, 186 Kennington Park Road, London SE11 4BT

e-mail acute@eauk.org

Website http:www.eauk.org

Telephone 0171 207 2105
           0171 207 2114

Fax 0171 207 2150

Foreword

Homosexuality may well be the single most divisive issue in the Western Church today. As acceptance of lesbian and gay lifestyles grows within wider society, many Christian communities have come under pressure to revise the traditional view that homosexual acts are sinful, and that practising homosexuals should not be ordained.

In the midst of all this, evangelicals are often portrayed as conservative reactionaries who are unwilling to engage in constructive dialogue. We must always give priority to God's Word written in Scripture and must always take the historic understanding of the Bible seriously. But we need also to recognise that the Church has at times expressed a hatred and prejudice towards homosexual people which has hardly reflected the character of Christ. In this report, ACUTE presents us with a positive contribution to the contemporary debate on homosexuality and the gospel. It clearly affirms the orthodox view, but shows genuine sensitivity to current pastoral issues. In doing so, it rejects homophobic attitudes.

I hope this document is widely read throughout and beyond the evangelical community, and that it becomes a valuable resource for all those concerned about homosexuality, the gospel and the Church.

Rev Joel Edwards
General Director of the Evangelical Alliance

Introduction

People may well ask, 'Why another document on this subject? Are there not more than enough already?' Much has indeed been published in the last few years on homosexuality and the gospel.[1] Some of this material has put the mainstream evangelical case, and complements the findings of a recent survey which showed that 96 per cent of Evangelical Alliance member churches thought homosexual activity to be wrong.[2] Even so, we are aware not only that many evangelicals face growing debate on this issue within their denominations and networks,[3] but also that some who still define themselves as 'evangelical' have begun to challenge the consensus.[4] It is against this background that we seek here to state afresh the classical Christian view of homosexual behaviour. In particular, our aims are as follows:

1. **To help Christians who hold the classical view to respond more effectively to the 'gay lobby'**, which by skilful use of the media and clear long-term strategy has won significant support for its cause.

2. **To help Christians relate more pastorally to homosexual people.** Evangelicals are sometimes accused of undue judgmentalism. While upholding biblical standards of sexual morality, we want to encourage evangelicals to relate with Christ-like compassion and respect to homosexual people, to recognise that there are such people

in our own church communities, and to speak with and about them
in a gracious and sensitive way.

3. **To affirm Christians ministering alongside those who seek to
   move away from lesbian and gay sexual activity.**[5] At present,
   formal UK ministries offering such help are few in number, lacking
   in support, and short of resources.

1

The Current Context

Homosexual practice has been recognised, and to various degrees accepted, in many cultures down the centuries.[6] Only in the past thirty years, however, has a significant proportion of Judaeo-Christian society come to see it as anything but a divergence from the moral norm.[7] Although more than two-thirds of men and more than half of women in Britain still believe homosexual practice to be essentially wrong, this must be set against a general decline in disapproval since the 1960s.[8] Across Europe as a whole, tolerance of homosexual activity is steadily increasing with each new generation.[9] Indeed, several Western nations face the very real prospect of those who disapprove becoming a minority. Insofar as they could be seen as opinion-leaders of the future, it may be significant that in the years between 1987 and 1994 the proportion of American college freshers supporting legislation to outlaw homosexual practice fell from 53.2 per cent to 33.9 per cent.[10]

This liberalisation of attitudes can be attributed to various factors. As we shall see, some have come to regard sexual orientation as inborn. Others have linked sexual expression directly to the principle of freedom of choice, and homosexual practice in particular with the autonomy of personal preference. For many, the move towards greater permissiveness on this issue has been less self-conscious or ideologically driven. Whatever the precise reasons in each case, it is clear overall that sexually active homosexual partnerships have come increasingly to be viewed as an authentic and quite natural lifestyle option.[11] Furthermore, this shift in public opinion must be understood as part of a much wider movement – a movement away from absolutes based on biblical revelation, to judgements based on self-determination, self-fulfilment and individual rights.[12]

Over the past four decades or so, an ever more powerful gay lobby has sought to gain acceptance of homosexual lifestyles in society at large. For Britain, a crucial landmark in this process was the publication in 1957 of the Wolfenden Report on Homosexuality and Prostitution, which proposed that it was improper for the law to concern itself with homosexual acts between consenting adult males in private. After dedicated campaigning, this principle was enshrined in law as part of the 1967 Sexual Offences Act.[13] Another landmark came in 1973, when the American Psychiatric Association decided to remove homosexuality from their list of 'disorders treatable by psychiatry'. This meant that they would cease to regard it as a pathological condition for which treatment was appropriate and healing hoped for – although they did keep it on a list of conditions which might occasion dysfunctional distress. What is not generally known is that this decision followed disruption of three successive APA Conventions by gay activists, as well as vigorous lobbying by the National Gay Task Force. The APA Board finally sent its members a letter which had been written and paid for by the NGTF. The APA's decision was not based upon any fresh analysis. Again, committed campaigning in effect secured the policy change.[14] Subsequent medical, sociological and popular consensus on this issue has been shaped by a highly motivated lesbian and gay community. The campaign by the gay pressure group Stonewall to deliver one million postcards to Prime Minister Tony Blair in November 1997 was just one more recent move in a well-coordinated programme of action.[15]

Throughout the same period, growing numbers of theologians and church leaders have responded favourably to the gay rights agenda. In 1955, the Anglican writer Derrick

Sherwin Bailey called for a reconsideration of traditional attitudes to homosexuality.[16] Bailey tried to distinguish between 'inversion' and 'perversion', and urged investigation of the causes of inversion, or what would now more often be called 'orientation'. Bailey's work opened up a discussion which was given significant momentum by the publication in 1967 of the Anglican theologian Norman Pittenger's *Time for Consent*.[17] Here, Pittenger argued for the approval of any sexual relationship which sprang from love, whether homosexual or heterosexual.

Just as *Time for Consent* reflected the 'sexual revolution' of the 1960s, so subsequent work by liberal and radical theologians has surfed the rising tide of that revolution. The years which followed publication of Pittenger's book saw growing acceptance of the 'new morality' espoused by writers like Joseph Fletcher and John Robinson – a morality which justified sex outside marriage so long as love was present, and which owed more than a little to the development of cheap, easy and effective contraception.[18] By attacking the established conviction that shared genital sexual activity was for married couples alone, this movement laid the ground for more recent attempts to reverse traditional church disapproval of homosexual practice.

Although general pro-gay sentiment suffered a setback in the 1980s with the spread of AIDS,[19] the Church appears to have bucked this trend. Indeed, the current willingness of certain mainline denominations to consider the ordination of practising gays and lesbians may well owe something to the understandable compassion generated among Christians by the plight of the many homosexual people who have contracted HIV and AIDS during the past decade.[20] Moreover, within the church itself it seems likely that some have been swayed by the pastoral qualities and work of homosexual clergy, who have felt increasingly able to 'come out' as resistance has eased.

For a long while, public perception in the UK typically associated homosexuality with single-sex environments where opportunities for heterosexual relations were limited – e.g.

boarding schools, the armed forces and prisons.[21] Today, such associations no longer dominate.[22] The widespread change in public attitudes can be attributed not only to the strategising of the gay rights lobby, but also to its allies in the civil rights movement, and to more sympathetic sections of the media.[23] The message purveyed through these channels is that homosexual orientation is biologically, psychologically and sociologically normal. This message is bolstered by its proponents' making the most of their opportunities to present gayness in a positive light; by portraying gay people as victims of injustice and discrimination who need protection, and by spotlighting instances of homophobia – that is, irrational fear or vilification of homosexual people. The common objective of such campaigning is to win over the 'decent-minded middle ground'. One consequence of this is that even measured Christian opponents of homosexual activity risk being branded as intolerant reactionaries. In certain work contexts, they may now also conceivably be disciplined on the grounds of sexual discrimination.[24]

The current legal situation is more fluid than ever. The Labour Government is committed to pro-homosexual reforms. It aims to repeal the law which bans the promotion of homosexuality in schools ('Section 28'), and, at the time of writing, intends to hold a free vote on reducing the male age of consent for homosexual acts from 18 to 16. It is also set to consult the Armed Forces about ending their ban on homosexuals. The projected incorporation of the European Convention on Human Rights into British law could also have a major impact in this area. Already, 'gay partners' have begun to seek the same legal and financial rights as employees' spouses, and in certain cases appear to be making significant headway.[25] Furthermore, Christian employers may even be subject to prosecution if they refuse to engage active homosexuals – although this would appear to contravene the UN Charter on Religious Freedom, which enshrines the right of religious organisations to make appointments appropriate to the 'requirements and standards called for' by the faith they profess.[26]

2

Key Definitions

In this time of flux, further confusions arise from the way people use the words 'homosexual' and 'homosexuality'. Often, they are taken to refer primarily to sexual orientation; indeed, some do not want to speak of 'homosexual' at all, but rather of 'people who are sexually attracted to those of their own sex'. Others explicitly mean genital acts between males. Others include lesbianism in their definition of homosexuality, and take this to encompass both female same-sex orientation and physical sexual intimacy between women. For some, homosexual practice would include non-genital contact such as kissing, caressing and holding hands – or even exclusive and emotionally dependent friendships between members of the same sex.[27] These more objective uses of the term have often been complicated by the cruder language of homophobia, which dismisses homosexual men and women as inherently disgusting or even hateful.[28] Moreover, confusion has arisen from inappropriate labelling of non-genital same-sex friendship, especially where two people of the same gender choose to share accommodation.

It could be argued that the traditional Christian stance has lost support partly because its advocates have failed to make a clear enough distinction between homosexual *orientation* and homosexual *practice*. We deal with this distinction more fully below, but it is worth acknowledging from the outset that the

Church's historic condemnation of homosexual practice has been heard by homosexuals of all kinds – including Christian homosexuals struggling to remain celibate or chaste – as a condemnation of *themselves as people*. Then again, it has often been lesbian and gay activists who have proved most keen to ignore the distinction – either because it challenges their view that homosexual people should have no hesitation about expressing their sexuality in physically intimate ways, or because it undermines their conviction that same sex sexual activity should be accepted as quite normal, regardless of the presence or absence of homosexual orientation.[29]

For greater clarity, we suggest that the word 'homosexual' be used of people whose sexual attraction is predominantly towards their own sex, *whether or not it is expressed in homoerotic sexual activity*; and that the term 'homoerotic sexual practice' be used to denote genital or other activity pertaining to sexual arousal between people of the same sex.[30]

While recognising that these definitions may not meet with universal approval, we would point out that there are problems of terminology on both 'sides' of this debate. Indeed, we note with regret the tendency of some gay activists to use the word 'homophobe' to define anyone who disagrees with their position.[31] We acknowledge with sadness that within the evangelical community, as in the wider church and society as a whole, there is still a significant degree of fear, misunderstanding, prejudice and even openly expressed hostility towards homosexual people. Where homophobia means 'irrational hatred or hostility' towards such people, we condemn it in the strongest possible terms and see it as a cause for repentance. We cannot, however, accept that to disapprove of homosexual practice on biblical grounds is in itself irrational, hateful or hostile. It is with these convictions in mind that we take issue with the Lesbian and Gay Christian Movement, and with others who seek to win the approval of the churches for sexually active gay relationships.

3

The Present Debate In the Church

Although the debate on homosexuality in the Church has
been developing for some time, it is fair to say that tension
has heightened considerably in more recent years. Within
several denominations, discussion of this question is now
proving very painful and divisive. Church members disagree
profoundly over what constitutes proper Christian teaching.
As we noted above, marked differences are beginning to
emerge even among those who would call themselves evangelical. Maybe it is inevitable that the rapidly changing
climate of opinion outside the Church has been reflected
within it. Whereas thirty years ago it would have been
unthinkable for clergy publicly to admit to a sexually active
gay relationship and remain in post, or for denominational
leaders to condone homoerotic sexual practice among ministers, or for official pronouncements from the Church to
waver from defining such practice as sinful – today there is
no such agreement. What is more, some denominations have
gay and lesbian advocacy groups, with priests and ministers
among their most vocal activists.[32] Society at large might
well conclude from all this that the Church, with its bitter
wrangling and uncertainty on the issue, has not only failed
to give a clear lead, but seems to have become increasingly
wedded to secular opinion. Some sections of the media
reinforce this perception with sensationalised reporting of

debates at synods and assemblies, and lurid headlines about
homosexual relationships among church leaders.

Challenged by such developments, it is hardly surprising that
many non-gay and lesbian Christians get confused. It is clear
that pastoral relationships with homosexual people – whether
neighbours, inquirers, or fellow church members – should be
marked by love and humility. But it is a common feature of our
fallen nature that even as we try to adopt such attitudes, we find
it more difficult to assert that homoerotic sexual practice is
sinful. After all, very few Christians wish to be perceived, or
described, as bigots. In addition, there have been much-her-
alded studies purporting to prove the existence of a 'gay gene'.
These have been widely discredited, but they have added to
doubts about whether it is right to condemn homosexuals for
a condition which some still claim is inborn.[33]

More generally, the fact that growing numbers of theologians
– some with an evangelical pedigree – are accepting that
homoerotic sexual practice may be legitimate in some contexts,
only adds to people's uncertainty. Such scholars often draw
apparently persuasive parallels between the 'liberation' of practising gays and lesbians, and the liberation of other oppressed
groups within society.[34] Among such parallels, one of the most
common is with slavery. It is argued that just as the whole
Church in time rightly responded to pressure from a minority
who contended that the abolition of slavery was required by
Scripture, so with homosexual practice today.[35] But there are
important differences between the two issues. The New Testament certainly treats slavery as a given – but already it
challenges even the comparatively enlightened way in which
much slavery was practised in the first century (cf. Gal 3:28;
Eph. 5:6–9; 1 Tim. 1:10; Philemon.).[36] No doubt there are
differences between the New Testament situation and that later
form of slavery which prompted the long battle for abolition.
Even so, Scripture contains within itself enough relevant teaching on human freedom and the importance of the individual
for abolition to be required by the direction in which biblical
instruction was oriented. A similar interpretative approach

applies to the remarkable liberation and dignifying of women which so distinguishes the New Testament from its immediate cultural context (cf. Lk. 7:36–50; Jn. 20:10–18; Acts 16:15, 18:28; Gal. 3:28). Like slavery, this is often cited as a precedent for the validation of sexually active lesbian and gay lifestyles.[37] But the truth is that when it comes to homosexual practice, there are no remotely comparable pointers to change.[38] Still, the parallels with slavery and the role of women are emotive, and to criticise them is to risk being seen as 'anti-human rights' in general.

Rights-based critiques of traditional Church teaching on homosexuality are certainly becoming more prevalent. Much contemporary morality regards any stand against homosexual practice as a restriction on free expression, free association, privacy and protection from sex discrimination,[39] and thus presents the classical position of the Church as archaic and oppressive.[40] Not only has this view motivated attempts by radical non-Christian groups to 'out' bishops and disrupt ecclesiastical meetings;[41] it has also begun to influence policy-making within certain church bodies. In 1985, for example, the Fifteenth Annual Synod of the United Church of Christ (USA) approved an 'Open and Affirming Policy' which enshrined 'the protection of rights without regard to . . . sexual orientation' for all its members. In 1988, the United Church of Canada followed suit.[42] While there can be no doubt from a Christian point of view that lesbian and gay people are entitled to the same basic human rights as everyone else, it is quite another matter to extrapolate from the protection of assembly, privacy and gender equality in society as a whole to the explicit *endorsement* of homoerotic sexual activity in the Church. Followers of Jesus Christ owe duties to God which may require them to lay aside moral options which the state defines as legally permissible, but which are nonetheless spiritually misguided. Despite this, both the United Church of Christ and United Church of Canada resolutions permit sexually active same-sex partnerships within their membership. What is more, they reinforce this by going one stage further and declaring the eligibility of sexually active lesbians and gay men for ordination.

Not only in North America, but also here in the UK, the ordination question has become a key focus of Church debate about homosexuality. In recent years, for instance, it has caused severe strain within the Church of England, the Methodist Church and the United Reformed Church.[43] In 1995, following a number of controversial debates at various levels, the Church of England Evangelical Council became so concerned that it convened a theological work group, which subsequently issued a 'St. Andrew's Day Statement' affirming the classical position that heterosexual marriage and singleness are the only two forms or vocations in which Christians can live a holy life.[44] Between 1990–93 British Methodists wrestled with the implications of a Report of their Conference Commission on Human Sexuality, and concluded only by setting a general reiteration of the classical view alongside an affirmation of the ministry of lesbians and gay men, and a devolution of decisions about particular cases to 'appropriate committees'.[45] In 1997, the URC General Assembly passed an 'interim' resolution allowing local congregations to ordain and induct sexually active homosexual people to ministry. By doing so, not only did it become the first mainline UK denomination officially to approve sexually active gay and lesbian clergy; it also alienated a significant number of evangelicals and classical Christians within its own constituency.[46]

These developments may indicate a liberalisation of attitudes on homosexual practice in the Western Church, but it is worth noting that at the same time, they have begun to provoke significant resistance from growing Christian communities in the Two-Thirds World. Recently, for example, the Anglican Churches of the South meeting in Kuala Lumpur issued a statement in advance of the 1998 Lambeth Conference in which they pointedly underlined traditional teaching on sexual morality and deplored homosexual practice as 'dishonouring to God and an abuse of human dignity'.[47] The tenor of this statement suggests that just as

Western Christianity is recognising and repenting of past cultural imperialism, it must beware of exporting a new form of ethical imperialism in relation to sexual behaviour. Indeed, we believe this to be a profound and salutary warning.

The many debates on homosexuality which are currently taking place in the Church highlight the diversity of approaches which underlie more general arguments about homosexuality and the gospel.

Broadly speaking, those who take the classical Christian view that sexually active homosexual people are ineligible for ministry are challenged by those who see the Church as being out of step with social progress, and as needing to modernise its criteria for appointing leaders. Some base this proposal on the premise that we can discount as culturally conditioned those portions of Scripture which define homoerotic sexual practice as sinful.[48] Others have said that it is merely the traditional *interpretation* of such texts which should be jettisoned – that the Bible, rightly understood, never pronounces against homoerotic sexual practice *per se*, but only against certain *forms* of such practice.[49] Others have invoked broader biblical prerogatives like love, friendship, fidelity and inclusiveness, and have proposed that these should override apparently more specific condemnations of homosexual activity within Scripture.[50] This last approach in particular has prompted an increasingly common distinction between 'faithful, stable, loving' homosexual partnerships and promiscuous ones, and has led an increasing number of individuals and churches to suggest that those engaged in the former should not be barred from ordained ministry.[51]

Reviewing the current situation in the Church suggests that Christians must grapple with certain core issues in relation to homosexuality. We must deal with questions of biblical interpretation; with homosexual origins and behaviour; with the historical dimension, and with practical and pastoral implications. It is to the first of these questions – the question of biblical interpretation – that we now turn.

4

The Witness of Scripture

General Points

The Bible was written over many centuries in several cultures
– all of them different from our own. But this does not
invalidate the abiding authority of scriptural revelation. We
see no reason why God should not make particular expressions
of his will within these cultures the expression of his perma-
nent will for *all* cultures. In any case, as we have hinted, the
Bible stands frequently *over against* contemporary culture. Both
Jesus and Paul are often diametrically opposed to social convention – on moral as well as spiritual matters (Mk. 2:23–8,
7:1–8; Jn. 7:53–8:11; Acts 19:23–41; Gal. 1:11–17). That they
are in agreement with their cultures at other points does not
invalidate this basic critical integrity.

Having said this, it must be acknowledged that direct
references to homosexuality in Scripture are relatively few.
Even so, they belong to a much broader context of biblical
teaching on creation, love, holiness and human relationships
– teaching which goes to the heart of God's purpose for
humankind. We shall deal with this broader context first, and
then discuss those texts which refer more specifically to
homosexual practice.

When God created the first man and woman, he was well
satisfied with his handiwork: it was 'very good' (Gen. 1:31).

The early chapters of Genesis do not go into great detail about the distinctions between female and male – but they do emphasise that each was a separate, intentional creation, and that they were made to be complementary rather than 'two of the same'. It is these chapters which provide the basic context for human sexuality, procreation and marriage (Gen. 1:27–8; 2:18–24). They are foundational for the Judaeo-Christian teaching that sexual intercourse is designed for expression solely within the life-long, marital relationship of a man and a woman.[52]

Of course, biblical models of sex, marriage and reproduction must be related in turn to the essential quality of love. The concept of love in the Bible extends far beyond sexual love. God's love defines our love, not the other way round: 'We love because he first loved us' (1 Jn. 4:19). God himself is Trinity – a community of persons in perfect loving relationship.

These principles are relevant to every area of our lives. They bear vitally on all our loving, and not least on our sexual loving. God's creation of the human race extends his love outwards and opens the way to a covenant of mutual trust and care. When God saw that it was not good for Adam to be alone, he created an 'other' – a woman – to be his companion (Gen. 2:20–5). The complementarity of woman and man is both physical and relational. They are designed anatomically for one other: they correspond genitally and procreatively in a way two men (or two women) do not. We are aware that this point has been dismissed as a 'naturalistic fallacy' – a leap of logic from 'what is' to 'what has been intended' or 'what ought to be'.[53] We also recognise that *heterosexual* sex is hardly confined to penile-vaginal penetration and reproduction. Even so, the link between heterosexual activity and procreation is more than incidental. Granted, the vast majority of such activity is not finally procreative; granted, God gave us sex for pleasure, too; granted, large numbers of men and women, who for whatever reason cannot produce children, continue to enjoy sex. Still, there can be no doubt that Scripture takes the procreative *capacity* of heterosexual activity to be a mark of its exclusive divine endorsement – something which validates it over against other, inherently 'sterile' forms of shared sexual practice (Gen. 1:28; 9:1–15; 15:1–21; Ps. 127:3).[54]

Of course, the complementarity of woman and man is more than physical. Genesis 1:27 emphasises that God created human beings in his own image – male and female together. The context shows that this divine image is expressed in a relationship which may be physical, but which is also spiritual, emotional and psychological. Man and woman are equally human (insofar as they have the same nature), but are nonetheless qualitatively different and complementary. Their being joined together as husband and wife becomes a fundamental expression of all this: 'So a man will leave his father and his mother and be united with his wife, and they will become one flesh' (Gen. 2:24). Here is the definitive pattern for human sexual love. We accept that this pattern was not immediately confined to *monogamous* marriage in the Old Testament, but would stress that monogamy emerged from it as its purposed end. Certainly, it is applied to monogamous marriage by both Jesus and Paul (Mt. 19:4–6; Eph. 5:31).[55]

It is clear, then, that biblical Christian teaching on sexual love would see it expressed properly in the lifelong relationship of one man and one woman in marriage. What is more, the Bible warns severely against disregarding this teaching, and hedges it round with laws and obligations designed to reinforce its status (Mt. 19:4–12; 1 Cor. 7:1–40; Col. 3:18–19; Tit. 2:4–5; 1 Pet. 3:1–7; Heb. 13:4). Indeed, the duties attendant upon husband and wife exemplify a principle which is often overlooked in gay and lesbian exegesis – namely that obedience to God's commands is not to be set over against Christ's rule of love; rather, such obedience is itself a mark of that love (Jn. 15:10; 1 Jn. 5:2–4).

While so much current debate centres on sexual activity, we should reiterate the key place in God's purposes of other forms of non-erotic love – e.g. sisterly and brotherly love *(philadelphia)*, and love expressed in friendship *(philia)*. A classic biblical example which illustrates both is that of David and Jonathan. Nor should we forget that Jesus chose friends whom he regarded as 'family' (Mk. 3:33–5). The closest of these were Peter, James and John, the latter of whom was distinguished as 'the disciple whom Jesus loved' (Jn. 21:20). These examples confirm that we need not be fearful of same-sex friendships. They should also spur us to reject insinuations that such friendships must involve homosexual activity. It has become a staple of pro-gay exegesis, for example, to present David and Jonathan in homoerotic terms – even though the text offers no credible evidence of this.[56]

Christians should be the first to insist that there are valid and honourable forms of love outside of marriage. Friendship between people of the same sex has been not only acknowledged, but acclaimed throughout the Church's history. The dilemma today is that contemporary attitudes make it increasingly difficult for such forms of love to exist without suspicion. This is much to be regretted.

It is important to note in this context that many homosexual people, for Christian or other reasons, are committed to chastity – that is, to abstention from genital sex. In this, they resemble many heterosexuals (whether single, divorced or widowed) who believe it right to refrain from genital sex – however much they may long for the full, physical sexual relationship offered by marriage (cf. 1 Cor. 7:11; 1 Tim. 5:9). In addition, of course, there are those of both orientations who have chosen the equally hard way of celibacy – that is, a lifelong, rather than a provisional, commitment to sexual abstinence. Not only did Jesus himself live a single, celibate life; he seems to have recognised and commended others who observed this pattern, even making a distinction between those (probably impotent but possibly with a strong same-sex orientation), who had been 'born' to observe it, those (probably castrated courtiers, but possibly others) who had been 'made that way by people', and those called to renounce marriage 'because of the kingdom of heaven' (Matt. 19:12 ... cf. 1 Cor. 7:7).

Specific Texts

The biblical passages which deal more directly with homosexuality have been expounded commendably by Thomas Schmidt, Gordon Wenham, David Wright, Mark Bonnington & Bob Fyall, Marion Soards,[57] and others (see Select Bibliography). What follows is essentially a brief summary of their work.

Old Testament

Genesis 19:1–29. No doubt the story of Lot and Sodom entails a gross breach of hospitality. According to justice and tradition, the men of Sodom should have protected Lot's visitors (cf. Ezek. 16:49), but instead they abused them. No doubt, too, the severe judgment of God which followed came primarily because of their idolatry, pride and rebellion (cf. Mt. 10:14–15; 11:20–4). This does not, however, detract from the clearly sexual nature of the abuse. The verb 'know' (v. 5) was far from rare as a metaphor for sexual intercourse, and Lot himself seems to have viewed the intentions of the men of Sodom as sexual by offering them his daughters instead of his guests, who appear to be men even though they are actually angels (vv. 6–8). Moreover, it does seem that in the New Testament, both Peter (2 Pet. 2:6–10) and Jude (Jude 7) regard Sodom's sin as at least partly to do with homoerotic lust. Still, the offending act is actually one of gang rape, which, as with the parallel incident at Gibeah in Judges 19:22–6, is all but irrelevant to the issue of non-violent, consenting homosexual practice. For a treatment of *this*, we must turn to Leviticus.

Leviticus 18:22; 20:13. These passages could conceivably refer to religious prostitution, and would thus hardly be pertinent today. But the thrust of both chapters 18 and 20 is against *all* forms of ungodly sexual behaviour – incest, adultery and bestiality as well as homosexual practice. All such practices are viewed as a threat to marriage and the family, each of which plays a crucial role in Hebrew religion. They are deemed wrong not simply because pagan Caananites indulged in them, but because God has pronounced them wrong *per se*. It is significant that when 18:22 commands 'You shall not lie with a male', it specifically prohibits men from taking the 'active' role in homosexual intercourse, even though this was widely deemed to be respectable in the ancient world as compared with the less acceptable 'passive' role. Also, the passive partner is here described using a generic term for 'male' rather than a more specific word for 'man' or 'youth' – something which further suggests repudiation of *all* types of male-male intercourse rather than just pederasty. Finally, the death penalty for homosexual activity in 20:13 applies equally to the active and passive partner: there is no suggestion of rape, in which case only the rapist would have been executed (cf. Deut. 22:22–5); nor is there any mention of coercion. The context, rather, includes mutual consent. The Assyrians may have outlawed forcible same-sex intercourse, and the Egyptians may have banned pederasty, but Israel stood alone in viewing homosexual acts *as a whole* with this degree of severity.

Gospels

Matthew 15:19; Mark 7:21. Jesus himself does not pronounce explicitly on homoerotic sexual practice, but then again, he did not comment explicitly on every ethical issue under the sun. Slavery and capital punishment, for instance, are not matters on which he taught directly. Having said this, his condemnations of *porneia* or 'sexual immorality' in Matt 15:19 and Mark 7:21 would almost definitely have been meant, and been taken, to include homoerotic sexual activity. Certainly, this was widely condemned by the rabbis of the time.[58] Then again, at least following the exile, there is very little evidence of such activity among Jewish men[59] – so Christ's not mentioning it in specific terms is hardly surprising.

Epistles

Romans 1:18–32. This seems to be a clear condemnation of both homosexual *and* lesbian sexual activity. In this respect, it appears to be unique among the religious literature of its time. Even so, some have argued that the phrase 'against nature' in verse 26 shows Paul to be referring only to those who temporarily abandon their heterosexual orientation for homosexual 'kicks', rather than to those whose orientation is solely homosexual.[60] The first problem with this interpretation is that it reads back the modern concept of 'homosexual orientation' into a text whose author would probably not have recognised it;[61] the second is that Paul's general focus is on forms of idolatry which contradict God's general intentions as Creator. In this context, 'against nature' is much more convincingly read as 'against God's purpose for human creatures *per se*', than 'against one's innate sexual orientation'. The same reading also counts against the suggestion, associated with L.W. Countryman, that Paul is here condemning only ritual uncleanness rather than sin as such.[62]

It is important to realise that Paul's *primary* concern here is not homoerotic sexual practice, but the more fundamental sin of refusing to glorify and give thanks to God (v. 21). Homoerotic sexual activity is presented as a *symptom* rather than a *cause* of this and, as such, takes its place in a whole list of transgressions (vv. 26–31) – a list which would convict most, if not all of us. Insofar as homosexual practice is highlighted at all, it is presented only as a particularly graphic *symbol* of the distortion of God's creation plan. Since Paul understands man and woman to have been designed for sexual relationship and procreation in marriage, sexual intercourse between people of the same gender becomes for him a stark outward embodiment of a spiritual reality – that is, the rejection of God's will.

1 Corinthians 6:9 and 1 Timothy 1:10. Some have argued that Paul is concerned here only with male prostitution or pederasty, and that these texts cannot be applied to committed, equal, long-term gay partnerships. But in each case Paul deploys a quite general compound word (*arsenokoitai*) when more precise terms for such practices were available. Indeed, this term is based on the Hebrew vocabulary of Lev. 18:22 and 20:13, and is used in subsequent literature to denote the *general range* of same-sex sexual activity.

Importantly for current debate, the context of Paul's remarks is eligibility for God's kingdom in general and for church membership in particular. As in Romans 1, homoerotic sexual practice here belongs to a list of sins: it is apparently no better, and no worse, than fornication, adultery, theft, greed, drunkenness, slander and robbery. This surely confirms that the Church is a community of sinners, and disallows the singling out of homosexual sin for special condemnation. It also suggests that early church congregations contained homosexual people, and that some of these may have still been sexually active. Even so, the clear teaching of Paul is that continuing attachment to this, as to the other sinful practices he mentions, is incompatible with authentic participation in Christ's new community: 'And that is what some of you *were*: but you were washed, you were sanctified, you were justified in the name of the Lord Jesus Christ and by the Spirit of our God' (1 Cor. 6:11, our emphasis).

General Reflections

It is always possible to pick and choose from Scripture to suit our own prejudices. Yet there are clear checks against this, and we would assert that the most authentic and dispassionate exegesis supports the Church's long-standing prohibition of homoerotic sexual activity. Of course, understanding the cultural context of biblical teaching is vital to its proper interpretation, but it will not do to abandon such teaching simply because we reckon our own context to be different, or because we are personally inconvenienced by it. To embrace such relativism is to compromise biblical authority as a whole. In any case, as we have shown, appreciation of the cultural context only confirms the classical view of the biblical witness – namely, that homoerotic sexual activity is wrong.

Even those who genuinely seek to justify their support of homosexual practice from Scripture tend towards special pleading. As we have observed, it is often argued, for instance, that Old Testament teaching on this matter is superseded by the New Covenant of love in Christ, and that Jesus himself significantly refrained from explicit condemnation of homosexual activity.[63] But this is too simplistic. The Protestant tradition in particular has urged a more nuanced approach to the interrelation of the Testaments. It has distinguished the civil and ceremonial laws of ancient Israel as no longer binding on Christians, from the moral law, whose underlying code is upheld by Christ, and so remains in force for the Church. The Civil Law related specifically to Hebrew society, while the Ceremonial Law was fulfilled by Christ himself, and most particularly, by his sacrificial death on the cross.[64] Certainly, Jesus appears to abrogate various Old Covenant commands. For instance, the civil penalty of stoning for adultery (which applied equally to homoerotic sexual practice) is effectively challenged by him in John 8:1–11. Nonetheless, he upholds the moral prohibition behind the penalty when he tells the woman caught in adultery, 'Sin no more'. This is one example of the basic hermeneutic principle of interpreting scripture by scripture (Mt. 4:5–7). It is quite different from abandoning any scripture which we find uncomfortable on the basis that it is 'culturally conditioned'. No doubt the civil-ceremonial-moral distinction is not always crystal clear, but it does seem to hold good in this case.

In short, we believe that the general pattern of biblical teaching on sexuality was well summarised by the House of Bishops' 1991 statement *Issues in Human Sexuality*, when it concluded that there was in Scripture 'an evolving convergence on the idea of lifelong monogamous heterosexual union as the setting intended by God for the proper development of men and women as sexual beings'.[65] In the witness of the Bible, sexual activity outside marriage comes to be seen as sinful, and homosexual practice is presented as a stock example of sexual sin.

5

The Witness of Science: Nature, Nurture and Behaviour

The actual word 'homosexuality' was first used only in 1869 – and even the root term 'sexuality' is a nineteenth century coinage.[66] The designation 'lesbian' has far more ancient origins – but etymology is only a rough guide to historical realities. We have already noted that, however it has been described, homoerotic sexual activity is well-attested across many societies, both ancient and modern. More specifically, it was widely practised and often condoned in the Graeco-Roman world of the New Testament and the early Church.[68]

What appears to be more recent is the entry into mainstream opinion of the view that some people are, by 'nature' (a word that requires very careful use), emotionally and sexually attracted to others of the same gender.[69] Although this 'essentialist' theory can be traced back to Aristotle,[70] it only gained real momentum at the turn of the twentieth century, through the work of Havelock Ellis, Edward Carpenter and others.[71] During the past hundred years or so, it has jostled for academic prominence with 'constructionist' explanations, which have assigned homosexual tendencies to social and environmental causes, rather than to genetic or neurological factors.[72] Indeed, more politically radical gay and lesbian groups now tend to favour the constructionist line: for instance, the founder of Outrage!, Peter Tatchell, recently condemned 'the flawed theory which claims a genetic causation for homosexuality',[73] while Darrel Yates Rist of the Gay and Lesbian Alliance Against Defamation has called the biological causation argument 'an expedient lie'.[74] Nonetheless, since the late seventies, the renaissance of sociobiology, which tries to explain human behaviours in terms of natural selection, has revived the essentialist case.[75] Faced with such a diversity of theory and evidence, it is hardly surprising that many have come to advocate more complex or 'mixed' models of causation.[76]

We have already pointed out a growing acceptance that the definition of homosexual orientation is far from straightforward. A whole range of factors may contribute to it, some of which may not be an individual's responsibility. It is possible that such factors might include a genetic or hormonal variation, which may establish the *potential* for developing a homosexual orientation. Even so, it is quite wrong to assume any 'automatic' causation from genetics.[77] Environmental and behavioural factors must also be taken into account.[78] Some have correlated homosexual orientation to poor relations with parents – and especially to poor father-son and mother-daughter relations.[79] Others have argued for a link with sexual and other abuse in childhood and early youth. The extent of these connections is disputed, however,[80] and the difficulties which attend the establishment of firm models for causation only underline the vexed nature of this question.

Despite all this, we would emphasise that the actual *expression* of one's sexual orientation is much more a question of individual choice. This choice *may* be influenced, or to some degree conditioned, by a mixture of innate potential and bad relational experience. But it remains subject to choice for the homosexual person, just as, for the heterosexual person, a decision has to be made whether to engage in sexual relations outside marriage. However we define our orientation, we must take responsibility for our actions. Interestingly, this point is accepted even by certain gay and lesbian activists: Rist, for example, is clear that it is 'cowardly to abnegate our individual responsibility for the construction of sexual desires'.[81]

These points become especially pertinent when it is realised that serious research into the origins of homosexuality has sometimes been distorted for propaganda purposes. For example, certain pro-homosexual literature still claims that 'between 3 and 10 per cent of the population are gay',[82] when the most recent and reliable statistics from the USA barely reach the lowest point of this range,[83] and when the most reputable current figures for Britain show that little more than 1 per cent of men and fewer than one in 200 women have had *any* kind of homosexual experience, while only 0.4 per cent of men and just 0.1 per cent of women claim to be *exclusively* homosexual in their practice.[84] Also, the renewed stress on a natural origin for homosexuality, which stems from neo-Darwinian determinism rather than any doctrine of divine providence, has nonetheless been seized on by practising gay Christians as evidence that 'God made us this way'.[85] The obvious point against such reasoning is that hypotheses about patterns in nature cannot so easily be related to divine intent: if we live in a fallen world, such patterns could equally be seen as at least a distortion of God's plan, if not a direct contravention of it.

Clearly, whether we are homosexual or heterosexual in orientation, we are called to conform our sexual behaviour to biblical standards. Distinguishing between homosexual *orientation* and homoerotic sexual *practice* leaves open the question of whether orientation relates primarily to genetics, or whether it has a predominantly social or environmental causation. Neither does such a distinction compel us to regard homosexuality as an entirely fixed 'condition' which must inevitably determine someone's identity and sexual behaviour. Indeed, this is borne out by the British research mentioned above, which concludes that 'exclusively homosexual behaviour appears to be rare', and that 'homosexual experience is often a relatively isolated or passing event' in people's lives.[86]

All this confirms that the main point for the Church is not to decide whether someone's orientation towards the same gender is 'inborn' or 'learned'. Nor is it to assess whether that orientation is stable or fluid. Rather, it is to deal with how people of whatever orientation in fact *behave*. No doubt all of us are finally accountable to God for our private sexual fantasies, as much as for our sexual activities (Mt. 5:27–8); but the Church has to frame its discipline on the basis of right behaviour, as much as on the basis of right attitudes and beliefs. Indeed, most Christians struggle with inclinations which may be genetic, or socially constructed, or both, but which are nonetheless defined as sins if we act on them. The problem, as we have already suggested, is that both within society at large and within the church itself, fewer and fewer people accept that homoerotic sexual practice is in any way wrong. Faced with this trend, Christians must assess it not only against the standard of Scripture, but also against the Church's tradition and history.

6

The Witness of History

Although the Church has consistently regarded same-sex sexual activity as wrong, mainstream Christianity has rarely stigmatised it as the worst of sins. Granted, it came close to doing so in the later Middle Ages, thanks in large part to the work of Thomas Aquinas, for whom sex itself was inherently sinful and meant only for procreation.[87] Granted, too, parts of early Protestant Europe imposed the death penalty for sodomy almost as readily as for crimes like infanticide.[88] But homoerotic sexual practice is hardly isolated for special treatment in the writings of the Protestant Reformers: they are quite convinced that it is immoral, but they do not see a need to discuss it at great length.[89] Granted, Calvin did at one point call same-sex sexual practice 'the most serious' of the sins listed by Paul in 1 Corinthians 6:9 and described it as 'that unnatural and filthy thing which was all too common in Greece', but even then he was quick to add that 'there is no-one in whom there is not some evidence of the corruption common to all'.[90]

Even as we get things into proportion, however, we should remember the overwhelming witness of twenty centuries of biblical interpretation and church teaching – namely, that homoerotic sexual activity is sinful. No doubt certain scholars today question the meaning and relevance of the biblical texts which deal explicitly with this matter – but previous commentators had little doubt. It is true that the early Church

Fathers scarcely made a meal of the issue. But this was only because they saw no need for a lengthy debate about something which they viewed as so obviously a sin. Certainly too, most remarks made in Patristic commentaries are brief – but this is only because their opposition to homosexual practice is so clear and incisive.[91] Having said this, when homosexual practice became a specific problem for the fathers, as it did for John Chrysostom in Antioch and Lactantius in Nicomedia, more extensive condemnations were offered.[92]

Before such condemnations are dismissed as having been conditioned by their time and culture, it is worth reiterating that the Mediterranean world of the early Christians was not wholly unlike our Western world at the end of the second millennium. Religious pluralism was the norm, and sexual freedom reigned – not least in regard to homoerotic sexual activity, even if it was not quite as respectable as it had been a few centuries earlier in Athens and Sparta. Roman emperors often indulged in it, and it was even thought compatible with being married.[93] So it was hardly an abstract matter for the Fathers. Yet there is no convincing evidence that the teaching mind of the early Church ever approved it.[94]

We make this point well aware that a very different reading of history has been offered by John Boswell. When first published in 1980, Boswell's book *Christianity, Social Tolerance and Homosexuality* made a powerful, award-winning impact.[95] Through radical reinterpretation of biblical texts and ecclesiastical documents, Boswell advanced the extraordinary thesis that during its first four centuries or so, the Church made no principled objection to same-sex sexuality as such.[96] Coming as it did from a Yale University Professor, this thesis was eagerly promoted by the gay Christian lobby, and is still cited favourably in certain pro-gay circles today. Yet in the years since its publication, many scholars in various fields have found serious fault with Boswell's case – for its selective quotation, its tendentious translations, its often bizarre definition of key words, and its generally inconsistent handling of data. Often, these detractors have had no Christian axe to grind: indeed, one of the sharpest critiques was published by the Gay Academic Union of New York.[97]

Seemingly undaunted by this, just before he died in 1994, Boswell claimed that liturgies for same-sex unions could be traced to the sixth and seventh centuries. Here again, however, his research begged more questions than it answered. Indeed, this later work was even more disputed on all sides. Still, evangelical Anglican Michael Vasey made much of it in his controversial 1995 book *Strangers and Friends*, which pressed for greater tolerance of homosexual practice in the Christian community.[98]

If it is true that the recent loss of consensus in the Church on homoerotic sexual practice owes much to a desire to 'keep in touch' with society, it should once again to be noted that the early Christians held several unpopular views in opposition to wider cultural trends – not least on this matter. Sure enough, Christian faith is tied inescapably to history: it is founded on an incarnate Saviour born in time and space, and on a canon of Scripture composed over a specific period. Nonetheless, it is also trans-historical, since the revelation of God which comes through Christ and the Bible both challenges and outlasts social norms and fashions. Indeed, biblical Christians should be in no doubt: the endorsement of homosexual relationships as on a par with heterosexual relationships expressed in marriage would represent a serious departure from the teaching of the Church throughout the ages, as well as from the teaching of Scripture.

7

Practical and Pastoral Issues

We cannot stress strongly enough that homosexual sin is only one category of sin among many defined in the Bible. *All* forms of sexual sin, like all other sins, are an affront to God and deserve his judgement. This point needs to be borne in mind when considering the vast amount of medical data on homoerotic sexual activity.[99]

In pragmatic terms, there is strong evidence that as a whole group, sexually active gay men put themselves at proportionally greater medical risk than sexually active heterosexual men.[100] Anal intercourse is virtually standard practice for sexually active gay men, but is very much a minority practice among heterosexuals.[101] This alone makes homosexual males as a group much more vulnerable to life-threatening diseases such as hepatitis B, neisseria gonorrhoea and anal cancer.[102] Also, it is a plain fact that in the West the percentage of those who suffer from HIV and AIDS is considerably higher among gay men than among hetero-sexual men, and that this is largely attributable to the prevalence of anal sex among such men, as well as to their relatively high average levels of promiscuity.[103] This all adds up to a life-expectancy for gay males which would seem to be markedly lower than for heterosexual men – and for married heterosexual men in particular.[104]

Insofar as Christians would want generally to promote health and well-being, we might cite all this as a reason to

discourage homoerotic sexual practice among males. Moreover, we might claim it as further evidence that such practice
goes against God's creation design. These kinds of argument
have a place, but they hardly reflect the main issue, which is
what God has revealed in his Word. Indeed, the risk-differ-
ential between sexually active *lesbians* and sexually active
heterosexual women is far less apparent[105] – and yet in biblical
terms, female homoerotic sexual activity is just as ungodly as
its male counterpart (Rom. 1:26–7). Besides, as we have
emphasised, neither is more sinful than heterosexual transgressions like adultery and fornication (Lev. 20:10–13; 1 Cor. 6:9).
We must, then, distinguish basically pragmatic arguments
against homoerotic sexual practice from more clearly theological objections.

We must also try as far as possible to ensure that these
theological objections are not clouded by homophobia. No
doubt fear and misunderstanding of certain sexual behaviours
can lead to undue stereotyping. A classic example can be seen
in widely held suspicions that more children are molested by
homosexuals than by heterosexuals. The facts are that most
sexual abusers are heterosexuals, that the *percentage* difference
between heterosexuals and homosexuals who commit paedo-
philia is unclear,[106] that a high proportion of sexual abuse
occurs within the family, and that some, to our shame, occurs
within the Church.

So we must keep homosexual sexual sin in proportion, and
be consistent in our arguments against it. Yet even as we affirm
this, we recognise that the high profile of debate on this issue
within the Church today has arisen largely because an active
minority has asserted that homoerotic sexual practice *should
not be viewed as a sin at all*. No doubt it is wrong to over-em-
phasise homosexual sin; but when such sin is re-cast as a virtue,
it is hardly surprising that those holding the traditional view
protest! Nor is it surprising that we should express concern for
gay and lesbian Christians who struggle to remain chaste when
more permissive voices in the Church appear to devalue their
chastity. Even as we protest on these points, however, we must

maintain an attitude of humble love and concern for *all* homosexual people.

It is a tragedy of our contemporary culture that God's good gift of sex has been grotesquely misused and cheapened. Over-emphasis on sexual liberation in the last three decades or so has gone hand in hand with increasingly secularised attitudes to abortion, divorce, adultery and family structures – as well as to homosexual activity.[107] In this climate, it does not help when some sections of the Church appear to reflect the world's priorities.

Having made this point, we would stress that the Church cannot afford simply to reject and vilify those who depart from its norms. The challenge is to return to a biblical basis of concern for the whole person: not just to proclaim that the brokenhearted can be bound up and prisoners set free, but to get involved in the binding up and the freeing. Jesus took a firm line on sexual sin (Mt. 15:19; 19:9ff.), but he was also a 'friend' of sinners (Lk. 15:1–10), and spent much of his time among those rejected by first-century Jewish society. Later, the Talmud collected together a large amount of material which confirmed that homosexual acts were seen by the Jewish community as sins, but which nonetheless urged that homosexual persons should be loved and welcomed.[108]

We have made it quite clear that to approve of homoerotic sexual activity is to depart seriously from both Scripture and Christian tradition. But from a pastoral point of view, it is essential to distinguish between approval of someone's behaviour and acceptance of them as a person loved by God. This, of course, can be a difficult distinction to make in practice. Many church members are not prepared for the discovery that someone they know is actively gay. This can result in a number of emotions – anger, grief, guilt, even panic. The discovery can also lead to a sense of loss. Security in one's own sexuality, and the relationship with the person now known to be homosexual, comes under threat. There is also often real fear for the Church's reputation. These responses are likely to become even more acute within those church families who discover that one of their number is gay.[109] In the face of all this, there needs to be a sacrificial approach – one which holds on to a relationship of love and compassion; talks rather than walks away; makes clear the biblical perspective on the situation; demonstrates mercy and forgiveness, and above all recognises that God is in charge. He is the judge, not us.

Just as Paul admits, 'of sinners I am the foremost' (1 Tim. 1:16), so we must see sin as a problem for ourselves as well as for others. At the same time, however, we must also recognise that God desires to save all human beings – those involved in homoerotic sexual activity no less than any other kind of sinner (1 Tim. 2:4). The Bible does not identify sin in order to drive people away from God, but rather to show the world its desperate need of the redemption accomplished by Christ, and to call people to faith in him. This redemption may lead on to a long and difficult process of sanctification, but the prospects for such sanctification are real: the success of those who help formerly active homosexuals on the journey may not always be spectacular, but neither is it negligible.[110] Those organisations which responsibly facilitate this journey deserve greater church support.[111]

The Gospel of Jesus Christ is a Gospel of hope and the Church is a community of hope. It is an organisation composed entirely of sinners. But insofar as they have repented, those sinners have been forgiven. They have been given new life, and a new lifestyle, in Jesus Christ. Repentance, forgiveness and re-creation go together.

In all aspects of the Christian life, and not least in relation to homosexuality, it is essential to balance biblical sexual morality with biblical grace in our response to every individual. Truth on its own can often be cold, condemning and occupied more with the letter than the spirit of the law. The heart of the Gospel is that truth finds its fulfilment in God's grace, offering the chance of repentance, forgiveness, and new life. Such truth is not compromised when compassion and respect are shown to an individual; nor are such responses a seal of approval on wrong behaviour. They are, rather, a sign of God's love.

It is with these convictions in mind that we make the following affirmations and recommendations.

Conclusion: Affirmations and Recommendations

We are conscious that different evangelicals might apply certain of these points in different ways, but we believe that, taken together, they reflect an authentic, mainstream evangelical response to homosexuality in general and sexually active homosexual partnerships in particular:

1. We recognise that all of us are sinners, and that the only true hope for sinful people – whether homosexual or heterosexual – is in Jesus Christ. Our earnest prayer is that his love, truth and grace would characterise evangelical responses to debates on homosexuality, both now and in future.

2. We affirm that monogamous heterosexual marriage is the form of partnership uniquely intended by God for full sexual relations between people.

3. We affirm God's love and concern for all humanity, including homosexual people, but believe homoerotic sexual practice to be incompatible with his will as revealed in Scripture.

4. We repudiate homophobia insofar as it denotes an irrational fear or hatred of homosexuals. We do not accept, however, that to reject homoerotic sexual practice on biblical grounds is in itself homophobic.

5. We deeply regret the hurt caused to lesbians and gay men by the Church's past and present hatred and rejection of them.

6. We oppose moves within certain churches to accept and/or endorse sexually active homosexual partnerships as a legitimate form of

Christian relationship. We stand prayerfully with those in such churches who are seeking to resist these moves on biblical grounds.

7.   We oppose moves within certain churches towards permitting the ordination of sexually active lesbians and gay men to ministry. We stand prayerfully with those in such denominations who are seeking to resist these moves on biblical grounds.

8.   We commend and encourage those homosexual Christian people who have committed themselves to chastity and celibacy. We believe that such people should be eligible for ordination and leadership within the church. Where they are members of denominations which are considering an endorsement of sexually active homosexual partnerships, we are concerned that they may feel seriously undermined.

9.   We call upon evangelical congregations to welcome and accept sexually active homosexual people, but to do so in the expectation that they will come in due course to see the need to change their lifestyle in accordance with biblical revelation and orthodox church teaching. We urge gentleness and patience in this process, and ongoing care even after a homosexual person renounces same-sex sexual relations.

10. We commend the work of those organisations which seek to help homosexual Christians live a celibate life, and also commend those groups which responsibly assist homosexuals who wish to reorient to a heterosexual lifestyle.

11. We believe habitual homoerotic sexual activity without repentance to be inconsistent with faithful church membership. Where someone is publicly promoting homoerotic sexual practice within a congregation, there may be a case for more stringent disciplinary action.

12. We would resist church services of blessing for gay partnerships as unbiblical.

Select Bibliography

The endnotes carry detailed references to material which may be useful to the serious student of this subject. Here, we offer a brief digest for the general reader. Roughly speaking, more essential texts come first in each section.

Studies Written from an Orthodox Christian Viewpoint

Schmidt, Thomas E., *Straight and Narrow? Compassion and Clarity in the Homosexuality Debate.* **Leicester: IVP, 1995.**

A Professor of New Testament Greek, Schmidt is excellent on the biblical material. Chapter 6 discusses a vast range of medical data, though Schmidt has been accused of selecting and manipulating this in a biased way. Overall, however, an invaluable source.

Wright, David, *The Christian Faith and Homosexuality.* **Edinburgh: Rutherford House, 1997.**

A concise but valuable booklet, especially sharp on the biblical material.

Bonnington, Mark & Fyall, Bob, *Homosexuality and the Bible.* **Grove Biblical Series No. 1. Cambridge: Grove Books, 1996.**

A 28-page booklet which does well to cover a wide range of issues – ecclesiastical, theological, exegetical and pastoral.

Soards, Marion L., *Scripture and Homosexuality: Biblical Authority and the Church Today.* **Louisville, KY: Westminster John Knox Press, 1995.**

Written against the background of debate in the Presbyterian Church (USA), this is balanced, and reasonably thorough.

Bahnsen, Greg L., *Homosexuality: A Biblical View.* **Grand Rapids: Baker Book House, 1978.**

An older book also from the Reformed camp. More conservative than Soards. Thorough on the biblical material.

Leal, David, *Debating Homosexuality.* **Grove Ethical Study 101. Cambridge: Grove Books, 1996.**

Helpfully challenges several stock presuppositions of the gay and lesbian lobby.

Higton, Tony (ed.), *Sexuality and the Church.* **Hawkwell: Action for Biblical Witness to our Nation, 1987.**

Still helpful compendium of essays by evangelical Anglican scholars. Contains particularly pertinent work by Gordon Wenham ('Homosexuality in the Bible') and David Wright ('Homosexuality in the Early Church').

Lovelace, Richard F. *Homosexuality and the Church.* **London: Lamp Press, 1978.**

A clear and concise survey of historic approaches from the early Church Fathers to 20th-century theologians.

Hallett, Martin, *Out of the Blue: Responding Compassionately to Homosexuality.* **London: Hodder & Stoughton, 1996.**

A shorter and simpler book, written by the Director of the True Freedom Trust. Winsome and sensitive, it reflects Hallett's wealth of pastoral experience.

Bergner, Mario, *Setting Love in Order.* **Crowborough: Monarch, 1995.**

An intensely personal meditation on Bergner's own healing from homosexuality, which draws broader inferences about ministry among homosexual people.

Davies, Bob & Rentzel, Lori, *Coming Out of Homosexuality: New Freedom for Men and Women.* **London: Hodder & Stoughton, 1993.**

Rather more of a 'How To' book, it assumes causes for homosexuality which might be debated, but like Bergner's text, contains many powerful stories and testimonies.

Payne, Leanne, *The Broken Image: Restoring Sexual Wholeness through Healing Prayer.* **Eastbourne: Kingsway, 1981.**

Again, a personal reflection, with guidelines for practical ministry among homosexual people.

Worthen, Anita & Davies, Bob, *Someone I Love is Gay: How Family and Friends Can Respond.* **Downers Grove, Illinois: Intervarsity Press, 1996.**
A practical guide, which takes seriously the possibility that homosexual orientation can be changed.

Other Christian Studies

Bradshaw, Tim (ed.) *The Way Forward? Christian Voices on Homosexuality and the Church.* **London: Hodder & Stoughton, 1997.**
A collection of essays from a wide range of viewpoints reflecting on the Church of England Evangelical Council's landmark St. Andrew's Day Statement. The contributions vary considerably in focus, depth and quality, but on the whole this is an excellent resource.

Vasey, Michael, *Strangers and Friends.* **London: Hodder & Stoughton, 1995.**
A controversial book, because Vasey has an evangelical background, but favours accepting and endorsing some forms of homosexual relationship within the Church. The first half attempts painstakingly to establish the 'social constructionist' view of homosexuality, but when Vasey eventually addresses biblical and theological concerns, he is far less thorough. Still, for anyone who wants to engage meaningfully with the current debate, this is pretty much indispensable.

Siker, Jeffrey S. (ed.), *Homosexuality in the Church: Both Sides of the Debate,* **Louisville: Westminster John Knox Press, 1994.**
An American collection of essays ranging over Scripture, tradition, science, experience and denominational policy-making. Traditional and liberal/radical scholars debate in each area.

Macourt, Malcolm (ed.), *Towards a Theology of Gay Liberation.* **London: SCM Press, 1977.**
In its time, a defining text for 'gay theology'.

Scanzoni, Letha and Mollenkott, Virginia Ramey, *Is the Homosexual my Neighbour?* **London: SCM Press, 1978.**
Liberal examination of various dimensions of the issue.

Countryman, L. William, *Dirt, Greed and Sex.* **Philadelphia: Fortress Press, 1988.**
Argues that Pauline prohibitions had more to do with ritual impurity than with homosexual practice *per se*. As such, it defines a view which has been much used by the lesbian and gay Christian movement.

More General Studies

Boswell, John, *Christianity, Social Tolerance and Homosexuality*. London: University of Chicago Press, 1980.

When published, Boswell's work caused something of a sensation, with its thesis that 'the early Christian church does not appear to have opposed homosexual behaviour *per se*'. Subsequently, critics on all sides of the homosexuality debate have had cause to question Boswell's sources and methods. Nonetheless, it is worth reading this as a prime example of revisionist gay church history and theology.

Greenberg, David F., *The Construction of Homosexuality*. London: University of Chicago Press, 1988.

If you only read one 'secular' book on homosexuality, read this. Greenberg is clearly sympathetic to the gay lobby, but he is consistently fair-minded and meticulous. When he discusses the biblical material, for example, he refuses to buy uncritically into the standard gay exegetical package. He manages to contain the comprehensive scope of his subject within a compelling, fluent narrative, and supplies an excellent bibliography.

Spencer, Colin, *Homosexuality: A History*. London: Fourth Estate, 1995.

More polemical than Greenberg, but a breezy, readable survey nonetheless.

Jeffrey-Poulter, Stephen, *Peers, Queers and Commons: The Struggle for Gay Law Reform from 1950 to the Present*. London: Routledge, 1991.

A revealing account of how gays have organised to shift public opinion and policy in their favour.

Addresses of Some Christian Organisations Working with Homosexual People

The Courage Trust, PO Box 338, Watford WD1 4BQ
The True Freedom Trust, PO Box 3, Upton, Wirral, Merseyside L49 6NY
Living Waters, PO Box 1530, London SW1W 0QW

Notes

1. For studies of comparable length and theological outlook alone, see Bonnington, M. & Fyall, B. *Homosexuality and the Bible*. Cambridge: Grove Books, 1996; Field, D. *Homosexuality: What Does the Bible Say?*. Leicester: IVP, 1979; GEAR (Group for Evangelism and Renewal in the United Reformed Church) *Homosexuality and the Gospel*. Southampton: GEAR Publications, 1993; Townsend, C. *Homosexuality: Finding the Way of Truth and Love*. Cambridge Paper 3/2 (June 1994), Cambridge; Wright, D. *The Christian Faith and Homosexuality*. Edinburgh: Rutherford House, 1997; Schmidt, T.E. *Straight and Narrow: Compassion and Clarity in the Homosexuality Debate*, Leicester: IVP, 1995. Official reports from church bodies include: A Statement by the House of Bishops of the General Synod of the Church of England *Issues in Human Sexuality*, London: Church House Publishing, 1991; The Methodist Church *Report of the Commission on Human Sexuality* Peterborough: Methodist Publishing House, 1990; 'Report of the Board of Social Responsibility of the Church of Scotland on Human Sexuality', in *Book of Reports (The Blue Book)*, General Assembly (May 1994). For other references, see Bibliography.
2. *Idea* magazine, January/March 1997, p. 31.
3. E.g. The Methodist Church debated this issue at length at its 1995 Conference; the General Synod of the Church of England returned to it in July 1997; and, after two years of consultation the United Reformed Church at its July 1997 General Assembly approved interim measures allowing local churches to ordain and/or induct practising lesbians and gay men to ministry.
4. Among those claiming evangelical identity who have nonetheless expressed openness towards homosexual practice, see Vasey, M. *Evangelical Christians and Gay Rights*. Bramcote: Grove Books, 1991, and *Strangers and Friends: A New Exploration of Homosexuality and the Bible*. London: Hodder & Stoughton, 1995; Atkinson, D. *Pastoral Ethics: A Guide to the Key Issues of Daily Living*. Oxford: Lynx, 1994, and 'Begging to Differ', *Third Way*, December 1995, pp. 17–20; R. Beadles, 'Us and Them', *Third Way*, December 1995, pp. 18–20. It is also worth noting that a recent publicity leaflet of the Lesbian and Gay Christian Movement identifies a sub-group specifically for 'Evangelicals'.

5. E.g. The Courage Trust, PO Box 338, Watford WD1 4BQ. True Freedom Trust, PO Box 3, Upton, Wirral, Merseyside L49 6NY. Living Waters, PO Box 1530, London SW1W 0QW.

6. For a thorough historical and sociological overview see Greenberg, D.F. *The Construction of Homosexuality*. Chicago: Chicago University Press, 1988. Also Spencer, C. *Homosexuality: A History*. London: Fourth Estate, 1995.

7. For accounts of the Judaeo-Christian legacy on this issue see Greenberg, D.F. *The Construction of Homosexuality*, pp. 12, 190–202, 218–34; Spencer, C. *Homosexuality*, pp. 52–65.

8. See Wellings, K., Field, J., Johnson, A.M. & Wadsworth, J. *Sexual Behaviour in Britain: The National Survey of Sexual Attitudes and Lifestyles*. Harmondsworth: Penguin Books, 1994, pp. 253–4. Much analysis of attitudes to homosexuality infers increased tolerance from the fact that younger people today accept it more readily than their elders – though this trend is clearer across Europe as a whole than in Britain specifically: compare Wellings, K. *et al*, p. 254 with Harding, S., Phillips, D. & Fogarty, M. *Contrasting Values in Western Europe*. Basingstoke: MacMillan, 1986, p. 122. The young/old contrast could, of course, be explained by conservatism growing with age; but the evidence for a more profound shift in social outlook is well corroborated: see Harding, S. 'Trends in Permissiveness', in Jowell, R., Witherspoon, S. & Brook, L. (eds) *British Social Attitudes: The 5th Report*. Aldershot: Gower, 1988; Smith, T.W., 'The Polls – A Report: The Sexual Revolution', *Public Opinion Quarterly*, 54:415–35, 1990.

9. Harding, S. *et al*. Contrasting Values in Western Europe, Basingstoke: MacMillan, pp. 121–6; Herek, G.M. 'Beyond "Homophobia": A Social-Psychological Perspective on Attitudes Towards Gay Men', *Journal of Homosexuality*, 10 (1984): 1–22. The interpretations referred to in n. 8 (above) apply here too.

10. 'College freshmen attitudes, 1994', *The World Almanac and Book of Facts* 1996. Mahwah, NJ: Funk & Wagnalls, p. 248.

11. Harding, S. *et al. Contrasting Values in Western Europe*, Basingstoke: MacMillan, pp. 121–6; Herek, G.M. 'Beyond "Homophobia": A Social-Psychological Perspective on Attitudes Towards Gay Men', *Journal of Homosexuality*, 10 (1984): 1–22.

12. For an analysis of this shift, see Davies, C. *Permissive Britain: Social Change in the Sixties and Seventies*, London: Pitman 1975, and 'Moralists, causalists, sex, law and morality', in Armytage,

W. Chester, R. & Peel, J. (eds) *Changing Patterns of Sexual Behaviour*. London: Academic Press, 1980.

13. For an account of the political and social run-up to the passing of this legislation see Jeffrey-Poulter, S. *Peers, Queers and Commons: The Struggle for Gay Law Reform from 1950 to the Present*, London: Routledge, pp. 8–89.

14. Satinover, J. *Homosexuality and the Politics of Truth*. Grand Rapids: Baker Books, 1996, pp. 32–7.

15. See Stonewall's leaflet, 'Equality 2000', dated 13th May 1997.

16. Bailey, D.S. *Homosexuality and the Western Christian Tradition*. London: Green, 1955.

17. Pittenger, N., *Time for Consent: A Christian Approach to Homosexuality*. London: SCM, 1967. (Third edition (revised and enlarged), 1976.)

18. Fletcher, J. *Situation Ethics*. Philadelphia: Westminster Press, 1966; Robinson, J.A.T. *Christian Freedom in a Permissive Society*. London: SCM, 1970. Cf. Dominian, J. *The Church and the Sexual Revolution*. London: Darton, Longman & Todd, 1971, pp. 9–16, 50–8.

19. Wellings, K. & Wadsworth, J. 'AIDS and the Moral Climate', in Jowell, R. *et al.* (eds) *British Social Attitudes: The 7th Report*. Aldershot: Gower.

20. This is explicitly acknowledged, for example, by Michael Vasey: *Strangers and Friends*, p. 239. Furthermore, the fact that the United Reformed Church became the first mainline denomination to appoint an AIDS adviser at its 1987 General Assembly seems, in hindsight, not entirely unrelated to its ground-breaking decision ten years later to offer formal endorsement to the ordination of sexually active lesbians and gay men.

21. On such assumptions and stereotypes see Jeffrey-Poulter, S. *Peers, Queers and Commons: The Struggle for Gay Law Reform from 1950 to the Present*, pp. 8–27.

22. But see Wellings, K. *et al.* whose recent study of homosexual behaviour showed that men and women who had attended boarding school reported a higher level of homosexual experience than those who had not, *Sexual Behaviour in Britain Today*, pp. 204–6.

23. For accounts of these developments see Jeffrey-Poulter, S. *Peers, Queers and Commons*; Greenberg, D.F. *The Construction of Homosexuality*, pp. 455–81; Spencer, C. *Homosexuality*, pp. 363–89.

24. On the growing inclusion of sexual orientation clauses in company Equal Opportunity policies, see Wintemute, R. 'Sexual orientation

discrimination', in McCrudden, C. & Chambers, G. (eds) *Individual Rights and the Law in Britain*, Oxford, Clarendon Press, 1995, pp. 491–533.

25. For example, the recent landmark case brought by Lisa Grant against South West Trains, which has been taken to the European Court of Justice. Grant cited SWT's refusal to acknowledge her lesbian partner of four years' standing as being entitled to the same travel concessions as the spouse of a married employee. At the time of writing, a final verdict had not been announced, but it seems likely she will win. For updates on other relevant 'gay employment rights' cases, see LAGER (Lesbian and Gay Employment Rights) website: http://homepages.force9.net/mysite/lager/news6.htm##CaseUpdates.

26. For a summary of concerns about this, see 'Religious Discrimination Fears Raised by EA', *EAR (Update Information for Evangelical Alliance Reps)*, September 1997, p. 4; 'Church Leaders Press for Human Rights Exemption', *Guardian*, 22/12/97. Compare: 'Declaration on the Elimination of All Forms of Intolerance and of Discrimination Based on Religion or Belief, 6 (g)', in Brownlie, I. (ed.) *Basic Documents on Human Rights*, Oxford: Clarendon Press, 1992, p. 108.

27. For the etymology of the relevant terms, see Greenberg, D.F. *The Construction of Homosexuality*, pp. 397ff.; Vasey, M. *Strangers and Friends*, pp. 9–10, 100–4.

28. On the etymology of the term 'homophobia', see Greenberg, D.F. *The Construction of Homosexuality*, p. 463 (esp. n. 39).

29. For differently weighted critiques of orientation-practice rhetoric, see e.g., Hallett, M. *I am Learning to Love: A Personal Journey into Wholeness*. London: Marshall Pickering, 1987; Vasey, M. *Strangers and Friends*, pp. 229–32; United Reformed Church Caucus of the Lesbian and Gay Christian Movement *Speaking for Ourselves*. London: The United Reformed Church, 1995, pp. 17–24.

30. For those seeking a more precise definition from a non-Christian source, Wellings *et al.* define a 'male sexual partner' as 'someone with whom a man has had oral sex or anal intercourse, or with whom other forms of genital contact have taken place', and a female sexual partner as 'one with whom a woman has had oral sex or other forms of genital contact'. For comparison, the definitional criteria for heterosexual intercourse include 'vaginal intercourse' and 'oral or anal sex', but do not include non-penetrative sex. *Sexual Behaviour in Britain*, pp. 213–4.

31. See e.g. Atkinson, D. 'Begging to Differ', p. 17.

32. For example, the publicity leaflet of the Lesbian and Gay Christian Movement advertises 'Groups for Under 30's, Evangelicals, Roman Catholic Caucus, Methodist Caucus (and) United Reformed Church Caucus'. The United Reformed Church Caucus's own booklet, *Speaking for Ourselves* (see n. 29) 'draws on the conviction and experience of members of the URC, *many of us elders and ministers . . .*' (our emphasis), p. 1.

33. E.g. LeVay, S. 'A Difference in Hypothalmic Structure Between Heterosexual and Homosexual Men', *Science*, 258 (August 30, 1991): 1034–37; C. Burr, 'Homosexuality and biology', in Siker, J.S. (ed.) *Homosexuality in the Church: Both Sides of the Debate*, Louisville: Westminster John Knox Press, pp. 116–34. For an evangelical critique and specialist counter-references see Schmidt, T.E. *Straight and Narrow*. Leicester: IVP, pp. 137–42 (esp. p. 137, n. 8).

34. E.g. Hibbert, G. 'Gay liberation and Christian liberation', in M. Macourt (ed.) *Towards a Theology of Gay Liberation*, London: SCM Press, 1977, pp. 91–9; Siker, J.S. 'Homosexual Christians, the Bible and Gentile inclusion', in J.S. Siker (ed.) *Homosexuality in the Church: Both Sides of the Debate*, Louisville: Westminster John Knox Press, 1994, pp. 178–94.

35. For a typical argument along these lines, see Vasey, M. *Strangers and Friends*, pp. 131–2, 136, 140.

36. See Reynolds, B.W. 'Slavery' in Atkinson, D. & Field, D.H. (eds) *New Dictionary of Ethics and Pastoral Theology*. Leicester: IVP, pp. 795–6; Kerr, W.N. 'Slavery', in Elwell, W.A. *Evangelical Dictionary of Theology*. Carlisle: Paternoster, pp. 1021–2.

37. E.g. Mollenkot, V.R. 'Overcoming heterosexism – to benefit everyone', in Siker, J.S. *Homosexuality and the Church: Both Sides of the Debate*, pp. 145–9; Hibbert, G. 'Gay liberation in relation to Christian liberation', in Macourt, M. (ed.) *Towards a Theology of Gay Liberation*, London: SCM Press, 1997, pp. 91–9.

38. On this point, see Hays, Richard B. 'On the redemption of our bodies', in Siker, J.S. (ed.) *Homosexuality in the Church*, pp. 9–10; Phillips, Peter M. *Dealing with Thorns: An Evangelical Approach to Divorce, the Role of Women in the Church and Human Sexuality in the Bible*. Sheffield: Cliff College Publishing, nd.

39. Drawn from the United Nations Universal Declaration on Human Rights (1948) and the European Convention on Human Rights

(1950), these are the grounds on which most 'gay rights' cases have been fought in the courts. For details, see Wintemute, R. 'Sexual orientation discrimination', in C. McCrudden and G. Chambers (eds) *Individual Rights and the Law in Britain*, Oxford University Press, 1993, pp. 491–534.

40. See e.g. Greenberg, D.F. *The Construction of Homosexuality*, pp. 467–75; Spencer, C. *A History of Homosexuality*, pp. 406–7.

41. For example, in a letter dated 30th December 1994, Peter Tatchell, the founder and chairman of Outrage! challenged the then Bishop of London, David Hope. Hope is a bachelor who has described his sexuality as 'a grey area'. Tatchell wrote: 'It is our sincere hope that you will find the inner strength and conviction to realise the importance of voluntarily coming out as gay and of speaking out in defence of lesbian and gay human rights . . . Your openness and commitment to our human rights could help precipitate a dramatic change in Anglican attitudes and policies. No Anglican leader has ever crusaded for lesbian and gay human rights. If you take this step, you will be doing something uniquely honourable and worthwhile' (Quoted in the *Independent*, 14th March, 1995). Later, in April 1997, Outrage! disrupted a meeting at Lambeth Palace when protesting against Archbishop George Carey's 'refusal' to support the 'right' of sexually active lesbians and gay men to ordination.

42. See Siker, J.S. (ed.) 'Appendix: Selected Denominational Statements on Homosexuality', in *Homosexuality and the Church: Both Sides of the Debate*, p. 205; Lesbians and Gay Christians in the United Reformed Church, *Speaking for Ourselves*, pp. 13–14.

43. For accounts and documents relating to the Church of England Debate, see House of Bishops of the General Synod *Issues in Human Sexuality*. London: Church House Publishing, 1991; Higton, T. (ed.) *Homosexuality and the Church: The Way Forward*. Hawkwell: Action for Biblical Witness to our Nation, 1987; Vasey, M. *Strangers and Friends*, pp. 207–10; Bradshaw, T. (ed.) *The Way Forward?: Christian Voices on Homosexuality and the Church*. London: Hodder & Stoughton, 1997. On the Methodist process, see Conference Commission on Human Sexuality *Report of Commission on Human Sexuality*. Peterborough: Methodist Publishing House, 1990; Vasey, M. *Strangers and Friends*, p. 202. On the URC, see Homosexuality Working Party *Homosexuality: A Christian View*, London: United Reformed Church, 1991; GEAR (Group for Evangelism and Renewal in the United Reformed Church) *Homosexuality and the*

Gospel, London: United Reformed Church, 1993; United Reformed Church, *Reports and Resolutions to Assembly,* London: United Reformed Church, 1997, pp. 45–9, and *Assembly Record,* London: United Reformed Church, 1997, pp. 10–13; also successive letters pages of *Reform* magazine from 1995 onwards. The Church of Scotland is somewhat less immersed in official debate on this matter, but see the report of its Board of Social Responsibility in *The Book of Reports (Blue Book),* General Assembly of the Church of Scotland, 1994.

44. Text and discussion in Bradshaw, T. (ed.) *The Way Forward?: Christian Voices on Homosexuality in the Church,* London: Hodder & Stoughton, 1997, pp. 5ff.

45. For a summary of the Methodist process, see Vasey, M. *Strangers and Friends,* p. 202. Also Conference Commission on Human Sexuality, *Report of Commission on Human Sexuality,* Methodist Publishing House, 1990.

46. *United Reformed Church: Annual Reports, Resolutions and Papers,* London: United Reformed Church, 1997, pp. 45–9; *Assembly Record,* London: United Reformed Church, 1997, pp. 10–14, 32.

47. The Second Anglican Encounter in the South, 'A Second Trumpet from the South', Kuala Lumpur, 10–15 February 1997.

48. E.g. Norton, R. 'The Biblical roots of homophobia', in M. Macourt (ed.) *Towards a Theology of Gay Liberation,* London: SCM Press, 1977, pp. 39–46; Lesbian and Gay Christians in the United Reformed Church *Speaking for Ourselves,* London: United Reformed Church, 1995, pp. 5–6.

49. E.g. Furnish, V.P. 'The Bible and homosexuality: reading the texts in context', in J.S. Siker (ed.) *Homosexuality in the Church: Both Sides of the Debate,* Louisville: Westminster John Knox Press, 1994, pp. 18–35; Vasey, M. *Strangers and Friends,* pp. 124–40; Countryman, L.W. *Dirt, Greed and Sex.* Philadelphia: Fortress, 1988.

50. E.g. Siker, J.S. 'Homosexual Christians, the Bible and Gentile inclusion: Confession of a repenting heterosexist', in J.S. Siker (ed.) *Homosexuality in the Church: Both Sides of the Debate,* pp. 178–94; E. Stuart, 'Dancing in the Spirit', in T. Bradshaw (ed.) *The Way Forward?,* pp. 75–8; Rominger, R. 'Ten Commandments for discerning the Word', *Articles of Reformed Faith and Religion,* Winter 1997, pp. 9, 11.

51. For examples of this approach, see John, J. 'Christian same-sex partnerships', in T. Bradshaw (ed.) *The Way Forward: Christian*

Voices on Homosexuality and the Church. London: Hodder & Stoughton, 1997, pp. 54–7; Vasey, M. *Strangers and Friends*, p. 208, and United Reformed Church Homosexuality Working Party *Homosexuality: A Christian View*, United Reformed Church, 1991, pp. 5–6.

52. For an exposition of this, see T.E. Schmidt *Straight and Narrow?*, pp. 39–63.

53. For a summary of this critique, see Vasey, M. *Strangers and Friends*, pp. 49ff.

54. For an elaboration of this argument, see Hilborn, D. 'For the Procreation of Children', in Durber, S. (ed.) *As Man and Woman Made: Theological Reflections on Marriage*, London: The United Reformed Church, 1994, pp. 22–32.

55. Cf. Vasey, M. *Strangers and Friends*, pp. 115–8.

56. 1 Sam. 18:1–2; 2 Sam 1:26. Cf. Vasey, M. *Strangers and Friends*, pp. 120–1, and Halperin, D. *One Hundred Years of Homosexuality*, London, Routledge, 1990, Ch. 4. But even Greenberg, who is usually more even-handed on such matters, resorts to speculating and arguing from silence on this point. He begins by admitting, 'In neither case does the text mention a sexual aspect to the relationship'. Yet then he goes on to surmise that 'an explicit homosexual relationship could easily have been deleted by priestly editors . . .'. So, for that matter, could much else which we should like to be in Scripture, but which does not appear there! Greenberg, D.F. *The Construction of Homosexuality*, pp. 113–4.

57. Schmidt, T.E. *Straight and Narrow*, pp. 29–99; Wenham, G.J. 'The Old Testament Attitude to Homosexuality', *Expository Times* 102 (Spring 1991), pp. 359–63; Wright, D.F.: *The Christian Faith and Homosexuality*, Edinburgh: Rutherford House, 1997 [1994], pp. 8–22; 'Homosexuals or Prostitutes? The Meaning of *Arsenokoitai* (1 Cor. 6:9; 1 Tim. 1:10), *Vigiliae Christianae*, 38 (1984), pp. 125–53; 'Homosexuality: The Relevance of the Bible', *Evangelical Quarterly*, 61 (October 1989), pp. 291–300; Field, D. *Homosexuality: What Does the Bible Say?* Leicester: IVP, nd.; Bonnington, M. & Fyall, B. *Homosexuality and the Bible*, Cambridge; Grove Books, 1996, pp. 12–23; Soards, M.L. *Scripture and Homosexuality: Biblical Authority and the Church Today*, Louisville, KY: Westminster John Knox Press, 1995.

58. For an in-depth study of contemporary rabbinical attitudes to homoerotic sexual practice, see Saltlow, Michael L. *Tasting the Dish:*

Rabbinic Rhetorics of Sexuality, Atlanta, Georgia: Scholars Press, 1995. Brown Judaic Studies, No. 303.

59.   Huggins, K.W. 'An Investigation into the Jewish Theology of Sexuality Influencing the References to Homosexuality in Romans 1:18–32'. Ph.D. dissertation, Southwestern Baptist Theological Seminary, 1986.

60.   J. Boswell *Christianity, Social Tolerance and Homosexuality*, p. 109.

61.   It is significant that Greenberg concedes this point, *The Construction of Homosexuality*, p. 215; see also Schmidt, T.E. *Straight and Narrow* pp. 77–83.

62.   L.W. Countryman *Dirt, Greed and Sex*. Philadelphia: Fortress, 1988, pp. 111ff.

63.   E.g. Wink, W. 'Biblical perspectives on homosexuality', *The Christian Century*, 7 Dec 1979, p. 1085; Lesbian and Gay Christians in the United Reformed Church *Speaking for Ourselves*, pp. 7–9.

64.   For a recent exposition and defence of these distinctions, see O'Donovan, O.M.T. *Resurrection and Moral Order*, Leicester: Apollos, 1986, pp. 159–60.

65.   House of Bishops of the General Synod of the Church of England *Issues in Human Sexuality*, London: Church House Publishing, 1991, p. 18 (para. 2:29).

66.   Greenberg, D.F. *The Construction of Homosexuality*, pp. 409ff.; Vasey, M. *Strangers and Friends*, pp. 99–104.

67.   See the extensive documentation in Greenberg, D.F. *The Construction of Homosexuality*, and Spencer, C. *Homosexuality: A History*.

68.   Wright, D. 'Homosexuality in the early Church', in Higton, T. (ed.) *Sexuality and the Way Forward*, Hawkwell: Action for Biblical Witness to our Nation, pp. 39–49.

69.   For a thorough account of the development of theories of 'innate' homosexuality, see Greenberg, D.F. *The Construction of Homosexuality*, pp. 404–11.

70.   Greenberg, D.F. *The Construction of Homosexuality*, p. 404.

71.   Greenberg, D.F. *The Construction of Homosexuality*, p. 411.

72.   Greenberg, D.F. *The Construction of Homosexuality*, pp. 411–31; Vasey, M. *Strangers and Friends*, pp. 10, 78–9.

73.   *The Times*, 20th February, 1997.

74.   Rist, D.Y. 'Are homosexuals born that way?', *The Nation*, October 19, 1992, pp. 424–9.

75.   A point stressed by Greenberg, D.F. *The Construction of Homosexuality*, pp. 432–3. For illustrative statements of the case, see, e.g.,

Wilson, E.O. *On Human Nature*. Cambridge, Mass.: Harvard University Press, 1978, pp. 149–53; Pillard, R.C., Poumadere, J. & Carreta, R.A. 'Is Homosexuality Familial? A review, Some Data, and a Suggestion'. *Archives of Sexual Behaviour*, 10 (1981), pp. 465–75; Kirsch, J.A.W. & Rodman, J.E. 'Selection and Sexuality: The Darwinian View of Homosexuality', in Paul, W., Weinrech, J.D., Gonsiorek, J.C. & Hotvedt, M.E. (eds) *Homosexuality: Social, Psychological and Biological Issues*, Beverley Hills, Calif.: Sage, 1982, pp. 183–96.

76. E.g. Byrne, B. and Parsons, B. 'Human Sexual Orientation: The Biologic Theories Reappraised', *Archives of General Psychiatry* 50 (March 1993): 228–39; DeCecco, J.P. and Elia, J.P. 'A Critique and Synthesis of Biological Essentialism and Social Constructionist Views of Sexuality and Gender', *Journal of Homosexuality* 24, nos. 3/4 (1993): 1–26; Schmidt, T.E. *Straight and Narrow?*, pp. 150–3.

77. See Schmidt, T.E. *Straight and Narrow?*, pp. 137–42 for a summary of the 'biological causation' debate.

78. Schmidt, T.E. *Straight and Narrow?*, pp. 142–8.

79. For a summary of, and references to this 'psychoanalytic' line of explanation, see D. Greenberg *The Construction of Homosexuality*, pp. 29–40. Also Schmidt, T.E. *Straight and Narrow?*, pp. 144–6. More specifically in relation to the concerns of this paper, see the work of Moberly, E.: 'Homosexuality: Restating the Conservative Case', *Salmagundi* 58/9 (Fall 1982/Winter 1993), 281–99, and *Psychogenesis: The Early Development of Gender Identity*, London: Routledge and Kegan Paul, 1983.

80. Compare references in previous note with Peters, D.K. and Cantrell, P.J. 'Factors Distinguishing Samples of Lesbian and Heterosexual Women', *Journal of Homosexuality*, 21, No. 4 (1991): 1–15; Lewes, K. *The Psychoanalytic Theory of Homosexuality*, New York: Simon & Schuster, 1988, and Robinson *et al.* (1982, cit. LGCM July 1997 paper to the General Synod of the Church of England), who showed 82 per cent of homosexuals as being in good relationships with their parents.

81. Rist, D.Y. 'Are Homosexuals Born That Way?' *The Nation*, October 19, 1992, pp. 424–29. Cf. Schmidt *Straight and Narrow*, pp. 137–42.

82. USA Human Rights Commission website on 'Workplace Issues', July 1997.

83. See LeVay, S. and Nonas, E. *City of Friends: A Portrait of the Gay and Lesbian Community in America*. Cambridge, MA.: The MIT Press, p. 102.

84. Wellings, K. *et al.* (eds) *Sexual Behaviour in Britain*, p. 183.

85. See, e.g. The Lesbian and Gay Christian Movement paper 'Facts DO Matter', sent to members of the Church of England General Synod, July 1997, which makes just such a massive logical jump having claimed that 'there is no doubt within the scientific profession that a proportion of male homosexuality is genetic in origin'.

86. Wellings *et al. Sexual Behaviour in Britain*, pp. 203–13.

87. Aquinas, T. *Summa Contra Gentiles* III, 122. Translation in Bourke, V.J. (ed.) *The Pocket Aquinas*, New York: Pocket Books, pp. 219–22.

88. Greenberg, D.F. *The Construction of Homosexuality*, p. 312; Abray, L.J. *The People's Reformation: Magistrates, Clergy, and Commons in Strasbourg*, 1500–1598. Ithaca, N.Y.: Cornell University Press, pp. 190, 219; Monter 'Sodomy and Heresy in Early Modern Switzerland', *Journal of Homosexuality*, 6, pp. 41–63.

89. For a summary of the Reformers' thought on this matter, see Lovelace, Richard F. *Homosexuality and the Church: Crisis, Conflict and Compassion*, London: Lamp Press, pp. 19–22.

90. Calvin, J. *Commentary on I Corinthians*, Trans. J.W. Fraser, Grand Rapids; Eerdmans, 1960, p. 124–6.

91. See the survey of Patristic references in Wright, D. 'Homosexuality in the early church', in Higton, T. (ed.) *Sexuality and the Church*, Hawkwell: Action for Biblical Witness to our Nation, 1987, pp. 39–50.

92. Greenberg, D.F. *The Construction of Homosexuality*, pp. 218–228 (esp. p. 226); C. Spencer *Homosexuality: A History*, pp. 84–91.

93. Greenberg, D.F. *The Construction of Homosexuality*, pp. 141–60; 202–10; C. Spencer *Homosexuality: A History*, pp. 39–78; Wenham, G. 'Homosexuality in the Bible', in *Sexuality and the Church: The Way Forward*, Hawkwell: Action for Biblical Witness to our Nation, 1987, pp. 27–38.

94. Wright, D. 'Homosexuality in the early church'.

95. Boswell, J. *Christianity, Social Tolerance and Homosexuality*. Chicago: Chicago University Press, 1980. Boswell's book won the 1981 American Book Award for History. *The New York Times Book Review* declared that Boswell 'restores one's faith in scholarship';

New Republic called it 'one of the most profound, explosive works of scholarship to appear within recent memory', while *Newsweek* called it 'an astonishing work of scholarship . . . [a] revolutionary challenge to some of Western culture's most familiar moral assumptions' (reviews all quoted in the paperback edition of Boswell's book, 1981).

96. For a clear statement to this effect, see Boswell, J. *Christianity, Social Tolerance and Homosexuality*, p. 333.

97. Johansson, W. *Homosexuality, Intolerance and Christianity: A Critical Examination of John Boswell's Work*. 2nd Ed., New York: Gay Academic Union, 1985. For other criticisms of Boswell, see Greenberg, D.F. *The Construction of Homosexuality*, pp. 195–6, 212–3, 212 n. 157, 213–4, 213 n. 166, 218–9, 229, 232, 288; Southern, R.W. *Saint Anselm*, Cambridge University Press, 1990, pp. 148–53; Edwards, G.R. *Gay/Lesbian Liberation: A Biblical Perspective*. New York: Pilgrim, 1984, p. 82; Wright, D.F. 'Homosexuals or Prostitutes? The Meaning of *Arsenokoitai* (1 Cor. 6:9; 1 Tim. 1:10)', *Vigiliae Christianae* 38, pp. 125–53.

98. Boswell, J. *Same-Sex Unions in Pre-modern Europe,* New York: Villard Books, pp. 74ff.; Vasey, M. *Strangers and Friends*, London: Hodder and Stoughton, 1995, pp. 82–6, 118–9, 212–3.

99. For an extensive bibliography of medical material, see Schmidt, T.E. *Straight and Narrow?*, pp. 222–36.

100. Cameron, P. *et al.* 'Sexual orientation and sexually transmitted disease', *Nebraska Medical Journal* 1985, 70: 292–99; 'Effect of homosexuality upon public health and social order' *Psychological Reports* 1989 (64): 1167–79; Cameron, P., Playfair, W. & Wellum, S. 'The longevity of homosexuals: Before and after the AIDS epidemic', *Omega*, 1994.

101. Wellings, K. *et al. Sexual Behaviour in Britain*, pp. 163–7; 218–227.

102. Judson, F.N. *Sexually Transmitted Viral Hepatitis and Enteric Pathogens*, Urology Clinics of North America, 11, No. 1 (February 1984), 177–85.

103. Wellings, K. *Sexual Behaviour in Britain*, p. 159, 213–8; Johnson, M. 'Social and behavioural aspects of the HIV epidemic – a review', *Journal of Royal Statistical Society*, Series A, 151, 99–114.

104. Cameron, P., Playfair, W.L. and Wellum, S. 'The homosexual lifespan'. Presentation to the Eastern Psychological Association, April 1993. See also Satinover, J. *Homosexuality and the Politics of Truth*, Grand Rapids: Baker Book House, 1996, pp. 69ff.

105. Lever, J. 'Lesbian sex survey', *The Advocate*, Issue 661/2, Aug 2, 16–24.

106. Freund, K. and Watson, R. 'The proportions of heterosexual and homosexual pedophiles among sex offenders against children: an exploratory study', *Journal of Sex and Marital Therapy*, 1992, 18:34–43; Freund, K., Watson, R.J. & Rienzo, D. 'Heterosexuality, homosexuality and erotic age preference', *Journal of Sex Research*, 1989, 26:107–117.

107. See Wellings *et al. Sexual Behaviour in Britain*, pp. 230–74.

108. Moses ben Maimon *The Code of Maimonides* Book 5: *The Book of Holiness*, Tr. Rabinowitz, L.I. and Grossman, P., New Haven: Yale University Press; Greenberg, *The Construction of Homosexuality*, p. 196.

109. For a helpful guide to situations such as this, see Worthen, A. and Davies, B. *Someone I Love is Gay: How Family and Friends Can Respond*. Downers Grove, Illinois: Intervarsity Press, 1996.

110. For examples, see Bergner, M. *Setting Love in Order: Hope and Healing for the Homosexual*, Crowborough: Monarch, 1995, and Schmidt, T.E. *Straight and Narrow?*, pp. 153–8.

111. See Note 5 above.

ACUTE is committed to an ongoing programme of research and publication on theological issues which are of concern to evangelicals. The ACUTE report *What is an Evangelical?* is available from the Evangelical Alliance. Forthcoming reports will deal with

- The 'Prosperity Gospel'
- Death and Hell
- Ecclesiology (the doctrine of the church)

For details on obtaining these reports as they appear, contact ACUTE (Publications) Evangelical Alliance, 186 Kennington Park Road, London SE11 4BT.

e-mail acute@eauk.org

Telephone 0171-207 2105
            0171-207 2114

Fax 0171-207 2150